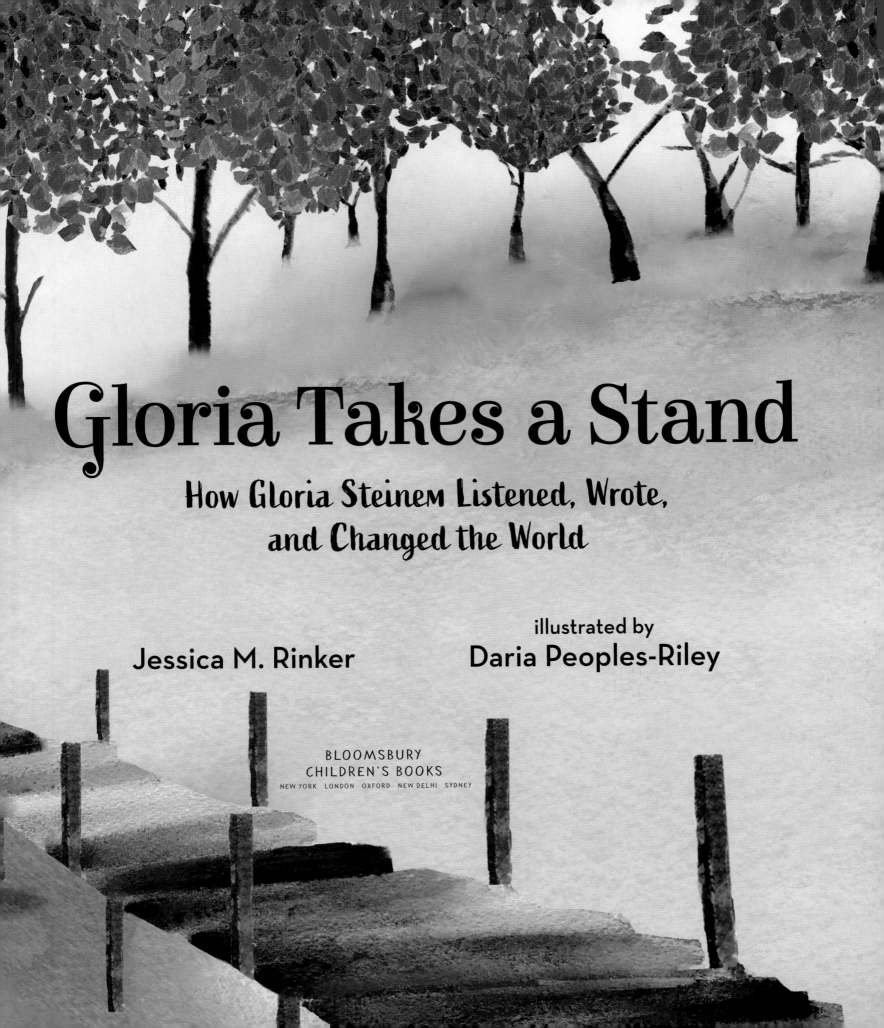

Gloria Takes a Stand

How Gloria Steinem Listened, Wrote, and Changed the World

Jessica M. Rinker

illustrated by
Daria Peoples-Riley

BLOOMSBURY
CHILDREN'S BOOKS
NEW YORK LONDON OXFORD NEW DELHI SYDNEY

BLOOMSBURY CHILDREN'S BOOKS
Bloomsbury Publishing Inc., part of Bloomsbury Publishing Plc
1385 Broadway, New York, NY 10018

BLOOMSBURY, BLOOMSBURY CHILDREN'S BOOKS, and the Diana logo are trademarks of Bloomsbury Publishing Plc

First published in the United States of America in March 2019
by Bloomsbury Children's Books

Bloomsbury books may be purchased for business or promotional use. For information on bulk purchases please contact Macmillan
Corporate and Premium Sales Department at specialmarkets@macmillan.com

Library of Congress Cataloging-in-Publication Data
Names: Rinker, Jessica M., author. | Peoples-Riley, Daria, illustrator.
Title: Gloria takes a stand : how Gloria Steinem listened, wrote, and changed the world / by Jessica M. Rinker ;
illustrated by Daria Peoples-Riley.
Description: New York : Bloomsbury Children's Books, [2019].
Identifiers: LCCN 2018024288 (print) | LCCN 2018037242 (e-book)
ISBN 978-1-68119-676-3 (hardcover) · ISBN 978-1-68119-677-0 (e-book) · ISBN 978-1-68119-678-7 (e-PDF)
Subjects: LCSH: Steinem, Gloria. | Feminists—United States—Biography—Juvenile literature.
Classification: LCC HQ1413.S675 R56 2019 (print) | LCC HQ1413.S675 (e-book) | DDC 305.42092 [B] —dc23
LC record available at https://lccn.loc.gov/2018024288

Art created with black sumi ink, gouache, and watercolor on paper, and then digitally composited in Photoshop
Typeset in Active and Neutraface · Book design by John Candell
Printed in China by Leo Paper Products, Heshan, Guangdong
2 4 6 8 10 9 7 5 3 1

All papers used by Bloomsbury Publishing Plc are natural, recyclable products made from wood grown in well-managed forests.
The manufacturing processes conform to the environmental regulations of the country of origin.

To find out more about our authors and books visit www.bloomsbury.com and sign up for our newsletters.

For Zachary, Ainsley, and Braeden,
three of my favorite stories
—J. R.

For the least of these—
May we listen to you in love and
fight with you through the fire
—D. P.-R.

When Gloria Steinem was a little girl in the 1940s, her family traveled all around the United States to buy and sell antiques for her father's business. Instead of going to school, Gloria helped her parents. From town to town they went, searching for sparkling jewelry, delicate bowls, and pretty plates.

Gloria watched.
She learned.
And helped.

One day, Gloria saw something she wanted for herself. She asked her dad for a nickel. When he asked what she wanted to buy with the nickel, Gloria said, "You can give it to me, or not give it to me, but you can't ask me what it's for."

You're absolutely right, Gloria heard. She also heard, *You're a smart kid!*

Gloria's parents liked how she thought for herself and could speak her mind well. Her dad gave her the coin.

Although she liked traveling, it was difficult for Gloria to make friends. Deep down she wanted a regular stay-in-one-place life like other kids had. She wanted to go to school instead of learning in the back seat of the car.

Then one day, Gloria finally got the house without wheels she'd been hoping for.

Gloria wished.
She read.
And imagined.

Her parents were separating, though, so her home wasn't as perfect as she'd imagined. However, Gloria made many friends living in her new town of Toledo, Ohio. She took dance lessons and loved school.

She spent a lot of time reading books by her favorite authors and imagining herself the heroine of the story. By the time Gloria was a teenager, she knew she would go to college.

But it was the 1950s and many colleges didn't allow girls to enroll. Gloria heard, *Education is a waste of time for a girl. Women should be wives and mothers only.*

Gloria wanted to go to college anyway. Her mother knew education was so important that she sold their home in order for Gloria to have enough money to attend.

She went to Smith College in Northampton, Massachusetts. In college there were ideas, books, and discussions about everything! Gloria was most interested in government. She worked hard and achieved top honors.

Gloria thought.
She questioned.
And learned.

As graduation approached, Gloria still heard,
When are you going to get married? She heard,
You should start a family soon.

But Gloria knew women could decide for themselves when to start a family. She said, "Decisions are best made by the people affected by them."

Gloria didn't want to get married or start a family yet. She realized she missed traveling. So, when she graduated from college in 1956, she decided to set out on a different adventure . . .

. . . writing and traveling in India. While there, Gloria saw people gather in villages and homes when there were problems to be discussed. They talked to one another instead of hurting people or damaging property—something they'd learned from a teacher named Mahatma Gandhi. They talked about their lives, jobs, and families. They made decisions together and came up with peaceful ways to make changes.

Gloria listened.
She watched.
And wrote.

She said, "If you want people to listen to you, you have to listen to them."

After she came back to the United States and began looking for a job, Gloria heard, *Some jobs are for women, but most are for men.* She heard, *You should be a secretary or a teacher.*

But Gloria wanted to decide for herself what job she would take. She became a journalist and wrote articles for magazines and newspapers. Everywhere she traveled for her job, people talked to her about their lives. Gloria listened to their hopes and dreams and asked them what they wished were different. She learned so much by talking to the people she met every day. She said, "Writing is the only thing that, when I do it, I don't feel I should be doing something else."

Comfort

by Gloria Steinem

The men in charge of the magazines wanted to tell Gloria what to write about. Gloria heard, *We want more stories about famous movie stars, big secrets, and scandals!*

But Gloria wanted to write about important issues and people trying to make a difference in the world. So in 1963, Gloria asked her boss if she could go to the March on Washington for Jobs and Freedom and write a story about Martin Luther King Jr. Her boss said no.

Gloria decided to go anyway.

At the march in Washington, DC, there were lots of men on stage who spoke about freedom and equal rights for people of color. In many places, black people were not allowed to go to the same schools, restaurants, or even use the same restrooms as white people. The huge crowds listening wanted to learn how to change these unfair laws. Martin Luther King Jr. inspired people to dream of a better world and to fight for what is right: equality for all people.

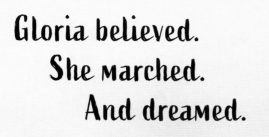

Gloria believed.
She marched.
And dreamed.

She said, "Dreaming, after all, is a form of planning."

Gloria heard the women in the crowd, too. *Who will tell our stories? The stories of mothers and sisters and wives and aunts? Who will talk about raising children and taking care of older parents and making enough money to feed our families?*

Not only were laws different depending on the color of a person's skin, women were also struggling to gain the same rights as men. They

didn't make as much money as men. They could be fired if they became pregnant. Women couldn't apply for checking accounts or credit cards without their husband's or father's signature. These kinds of restrictions made it impossible for women to take care of themselves.

No one was listening.

But Gloria was listening. People of color are not less important than white people and women are not less important than men. Gloria said, "Imagine we are linked not ranked."

As the 1970s approached, things were beginning to change slowly, but women still faced opposition. They were tired of hearing what other people thought they should do. Women needed a safe place to speak. So Gloria decided to do something about it.

In 1971, Gloria started *Ms.* magazine with her friend Dorothy Pitman Hughes. *Ms.* was the first magazine owned and written by women. Now women could write and read about the topics that were important to them.

    Ms. published articles about women who were changing laws, making choices for their own bodies, and protecting themselves from violence. There were articles about protests and poetry and art. There were stories about female astronauts, secretaries, and even Wonder Woman! Women wanted a better world for women. *Ms.* magazine helped.

Gloria paid attention.
She planned.
And spoke.

Gloria began organizing groups for women to talk about the changes they needed, just like she had seen in India when people gathered. She believed, "Girls need to know they can break the rules."

This became known as the women's liberation movement, and the women and men involved were called feminists. A feminist believes that all people should have equal opportunities. Gloria said, "Feminism . . . is about making life more fair for women everywhere." People looked to Gloria as one of the leaders of the movement, and they wanted her to speak around the country!

At first it was scary for Gloria to speak in front of large groups of people. But she always had other women with her, like her friend Dorothy. Another woman who traveled and spoke to women with Gloria was her friend Bella Abzug. Bella was a congresswoman, lawyer, and feminist. Like Gloria, Bella was also fighting for change. Each woman had important issues to talk about; together they could reach more people.

When it was Gloria's turn on stage, she didn't feel alone. She thought about all the women she'd met during her trips, all the stories she'd read in her magazine, and all of the amazing jobs women were doing now. Poets, politicians, doctors, mothers, lawyers, activists, homemakers. Their stories were all within her. Their stories made her strong.

Gloria remembered.
She stood.
And shouted!

Gloria said, "The future depends entirely on what each of us does every day."

Because of all the work Gloria and other feminists did, today girls hear:

BLACK LIVES MATTER
DO YOU WANT TO HAVE CHILDREN?
What kind of changes do you want to make?
BE YOURSELF
The Future is YOURS!

Gloria doesn't travel as much as she once did, but she still fights for equal rights for all women, for all people.

Gloria still writes.
She still speaks.
And still listens.

And she still wants girls and boys to stand up and speak for equal rights for all people.

Author's Note

When I attended college in the nineties, my major was social welfare. I loved studying social issues, psychology, history—all the subjects that explained why people do what they do. But women's studies as a discipline wasn't as robust as it is now, and so most of these classes revolved around the work men had done. All I knew of Gloria at that time was that she was considered a controversial figure for her support of women's rights. I never had the chance to study her activism or the women's movement in school, and I didn't learn more about it on my own until much later in life. But when I began reading Gloria's books, it blew open a door to a whole new world for me! I became aware of just how much work women—and especially African American women—have done to help our country reach the point of where we are now.

Gloria's work speaks for itself. I used a few resources written by others, but I focused on her words: her books and articles, her powerful talks and lectures. In this story for the youngest readers, I tried to let Gloria speak for herself because I want those who read her story to grow up knowing whoever they are is just fine and learning how to make change: by listening, dreaming, and speaking.

What amazes me the most about Gloria is that she saw and heard the expectations many people had about women but she had her own ideas about how to live her life. This independent thinking on her part, as well as other women of the time, is what began a revolution.

The choices she made contributed to the creation of the women's movement, which helped all women gain the ability to make their own choices as well.

After college, Gloria wanted to travel and write, and she would go on to publish hundreds of articles and several books. She also won many awards for her work as a writer and as an activist, including the Presidential Medal of Freedom in 2013.

All of this work comprised the activism for which she is now an icon. But Gloria would be the first to say that she did not do this alone. Many women fought hard. Many women spoke and wrote and changed laws. Together, women from many races and backgrounds pioneered feminism.

Women won the right to vote in 1920, which was before Gloria's time, but there was still so much women were not allowed to do when Gloria was growing up.

As a direct result of Gloria's and other feminists' efforts, these changes have given women more equality and freedom. However, there are still ways in which not all people are equal. Part of change is creating new and better laws. But the other part of change is helping people understand why new and better laws are needed in the first place.

Feminists show that it's up to each of us to decide what we want to be and do with our lives. They fight for the right of all people to marry who they want; to have children when they want; and to be able to live, shop, and work wherever they choose.

There are so many stories of women who have been part of this great movement. Gloria became the voice of all the women she met, the writer of many important stories. Gloria's story is only one.

But it's a good one.

Illustrator's Note

To capture the essence of Gloria Steinem's life's work and reimagine her journey for young readers, I relied strongly on the power of her words to inform my creative decisions. In her book *My Life on the Road*, she shares the foundation of her legacy, invaluable wisdom for all who wish to change the world. Ms. Steinem writes, "If you want people to listen to you, you have to listen to them. If you hope people will change how they live, you have to know how they live. If you want people to see you, you have to sit down with them eye-to-eye."

While reflecting on all that Ms. Steinem achieved, I imagined the world through her eyes to be colorful, vivid, and hopeful. In my illustrations for *Gloria Takes a Stand*, bright skies surround her during marches and protests,

as if the universe champions her work amid the struggle.

Ms. Steinem listened when others ignored, so in many illustrations I drew her standing to the side, as observers do. She spoke out when others were silent—even at the cost of not being admired. So I made sure her expressions were strong and confident, but her eyes revealed hints of concern.

Ms. Steinem remains unwavering in her dedication to excavating the untold stories of others. Her work in the women's liberation movement has given all women permission to seek individual freedom. With the help of many women and men who joined her cause, Ms. Steinem's journey empowers us to use our voices and our actions to become the best versions of ourselves.

Important Events in US Women's History

© MICHAEL OCHES ARCHIVES/GETTY IMAGES

1900

1890 · Wyoming is the first state to grant women the right to vote. Other states still consider women to be a "special category of nonvoting citizens."

1920 · The Nineteenth Amendment allows women in all states to vote.

1920

1938 · The Fair Labor Standards Act establishes a minimum wage for many workers.

1940

1960 · The FDA approves oral birth control for general use, allowing women to request prescriptions.

1964 · Title VII of the Civil Rights Act passes. The act includes a prohibition against employment discrimination on the basis of race, color, religion, national origin, or sex.

1972 · Title IX of the Education Amendments is passed, protecting people from discrimination based on sex in all educational programs or activities that receive funding from the federal government.

1960

1973 · The court case *Roe v. Wade* establishes the right to abortion.

1974 · The Equal Credit Opportunity Act prohibits banks from discrimination against women.

1975 · States may not exclude women from serving on a jury.

1980

1978 · The Pregnancy Discrimination Act is passed, making it illegal for an employer to dismiss a woman if she becomes pregnant.

1981 · The Supreme Court decides Louisiana's property laws are unconstitutional, allowing women in all states to be equal property owners with their spouses.

1983 · Columbia University is the last Ivy League college to admit women.

1984 · Mississippi belatedly ratifies the Nineteenth Amendment, acknowledging that a woman's right to vote is a state as well as a federal right for women voters in that state.

2000

1994 · Congress passes the Violence Against Women Act of 1994 to combat violence and crimes against women.

2013 · Women are allowed to fill military combat roles.

Bibliography

BOOKS

Fabiny, Sarah, with illustrations by Max Hergenrother. *Who Is Gloria Steinem?*, New York: Grosset & Dunlap, 2014.

Heilbrun, Carolyn G. *The Education of a Woman: The Life of Gloria Steinem*, New York: Ballantine Books, 1995.

Steinem, Gloria. *My Life on the Road*, New York: Random House, 2016.

——. *Outrageous Acts and Everyday Rebellions*, New York: Henry Holt and Company, 1995.

——. *Revolution from Within*, Boston: Little, Brown, 1992.

Thom, Mary. *Inside Ms.: 25 Years of the Magazine and the Feminist Movement*, New York: Henry Holt, 1998.

BROADCAST AND OTHER MEDIA

Gloria: In Her Own Words (HBO)

Gloriasteinem.com

Makers: Women Who Make America, Gloria Steinem (PBS)

QUOTATION SOURCES

"You can give it to me": *My Life on the Road*, 21

"Decisions are best made": *My Life on the Road*, 39

"If you want people to listen to you": *My Life on the Road*, 37

"Writing is the only thing": www.gloriasteinem.com/written-works

"Dreaming, after all": www.gloriasteinem.com/news

"Imagine we are linked": www.gloriasteinem.com

"Girls need to know": *My Life on the Road*, 79

"Feminism . . . is about making": *Los Angeles Times*, articles.latimes.com/2008/sep/04/news /OE-STEINEM4

"The future depends": www.gloriasteinem.com/contact

WOMEN FEATURED ON THE ENDPAPERS: *Top row:* Betty Friedan, Dolores Huerta, Michele Wallace, Dorothy Pitman Hughes, Alice Walker, Margaret Sloan-Hunter; *Bottom row:* Maya Angelou, Coretta Scott King, Bella Abzug, Florynce Kennedy, Cicely Tyson, Hillary Rodham Clinton.